WENDY HYDE

DECORATING
for REAL LIFE

THE SHABBY NEST'S GUIDE
TO BEAUTIFUL, FAMILY-FRIENDLY SPACES

PLAIN SIGHT PUBLISHING
AN IMPRINT OF CEDAR FORT, INC.
SPRINGVILLE, UTAH

ISBN 13: 978-1-4621-1412-2

Published by Plain Sight Publishing, an imprint of Cedar Fort, Inc.
2373 W. 700 S., Springville, UT 84663
Distributed by Cedar Fort, Inc., www.cedarfort.com

LIBRARY OF CONGRESS CATALOGING-IN-PUBLICATION DATA

Hyde, Wendy W., 1972- author.
Decorating for real life : the Shabby Nest's guide to beautiful family friendly spaces / Wendy W. Hyde.
  pages cm
Includes bibliographical references and index.
Summary: Includes DIY projects and ideas for the home.
ISBN 978-1-4621-1412-2 (alk. paper)
1. Interior decoration. I. Title.

NK2110.H93 2014
747--dc23

2014018492

Cover and page design by Angela D. Baxter
Cover design © 2014 by Lyle Mortimer
Edited by Deborah Spencer

Printed in China

10 9 8 7 6 5 4 3 2 1

Printed on acid-free paper

5600 1901
3/15

DEDICATION

For my family, who provide me
with my greatest inspiration.

CONTENTS

9

29

CHARMING & CHEERFUL

CURATED & CULTIVATED

49

63

83

COZY & COMFORTABLE

COOL & CURRENT

PETITE & PRETTY

97

117

131

LUXE & LIVABLE

BRIGHT & BEACHY

SIMPLE & SERENE

FRESH & FABULOUS

GLOBAL & GLAM

CLEAN & CONTEMPORARY

"I'M GOING TO MAKE EVERYTHING AROUND
ME BEAUTIFUL—THAT WILL BE MY LIFE."

ELSIE DE WOLFE

INTRODUCTION

DOES YOUR HOUSE talk to you?

Mine does.

Okay, before you go thinking that I might need a little therapy, I'm not hearing actual voices. But when I walk into a house, it has a way of telling me how it should be decorated. If you love decorating as much as I do, you know what I'm talking about. Houses just have a certain feeling to them independent of their inhabitants. Finding a way to combine your home's language with your own voice is what interior design is all about. It is about the combination of a structure with four walls and the personal expression of an individual.

Finding your own decorating voice within a space is the fun part. A house is more than just a roof and plaster walls. It is more than just shelter. A house is the raw material from which we build a home. And home is the genesis of everything that is important to us. It is the launching pad from which our children go forth into the world, and it is the safe haven to which they return. It is the place we regroup, the place we relax, the place we retreat. Because home plays all of these central roles in our lives, it is important that we make it a place that we enjoy being.

It is my philosophy that our homes should be places we love. They should be a reflection of who we are both as individuals and as families. They should make a statement about the things we value, the things we find beautiful, and the things that make us smile.

As a designer, I have heard many clients say that they'd love to have certain items in their homes, but that they will need to wait until their children are grown. As the mother of four myself, I understand the concern behind this statement. But the problem with the idea of waiting until your children are grown is that I also hear older clients say that they'd love to decorate their homes in a certain way, but they have grandchildren, so they will have to wait until those grandchildren are grown.

If we are always waiting for something to change before we create the type of home we long for, we will never get to live in that dream home. I wholeheartedly believe that a home can be family friendly, completely functional, and beautiful all at the same time. All it takes is ingenuity, creativity, and perhaps a bit of compromise, but it can be done.

In this book, I will share amazing real-life spaces. All of them are inhabited by families, most of whom have young children. All of them are lived in, and I mean *lived in*. And each of them showcases my theory in distinct and beautiful ways. I hope that these houses will inspire you with practical ideas for real-life decorating that will make your house more than just a house. It is my hope that this book will be an interactive guide to creating rooms that are eloquent but quirky, full of personality, beautiful, and distinctively individual, and that it will help you make your house into the home of your dreams.

DECORATING 101

OUR HOMES ARE important in that they are the places where we nurture our family. They are the places that we want our family to be together in, to learn in, to grow in and to feel love in. Making a beautiful home extends far beyond wanting a space to be magazine-worthy. Making a beautiful home is a love language. It is a love language that we have for ourselves, for our families, and for our friends. It is one way that we show those closest to us that we care about them. By creating inviting spaces, we welcome family and friends and show them that we want to have them near us and to enjoy being in our homes.

With this ideal as a background, the concept of creating a beautiful home becomes a labor of love as well as a creative outlet.

I am not a hard and fast rule follower when it comes to decorating. And beautiful spaces can definitely be created without following a specific formula and without obeying any particular rules of decorating. However, having a plan and knowing some of the fundamentals of interior design will save time, money, and frustration when you are in the process of creating your home.

So let's start with a few of the basic concepts of interior design. We'll call this little lesson Decorating 101.

Creating a beautiful home doesn't just happen. To create a successful space you always need to have a plan. Creating a plan to work from will make the entire process simpler. And it will go a long way toward making sure your house becomes a place that you love.

SPACE PLANNING

Whether you are a family of one or a family of ten, efficient use of space is the most important aspect of designing a home. When a house doesn't flow, or the space is configured awkwardly, that feeling can be internalized, and the occupants feel awkward in the space no matter how beautifully it is decorated. Remember when I talked about houses telling me how they want to be decorated? One of the first things they tell me is how the space should be configured. And truthfully, space planning should be the first step in decorating any room.

Very few houses are built with perfectly dimensioned rooms that work well with anything you might put in them. Even fewer houses fall naturally into the flow of how you and your family live. Figuring out how your family will live within a space and then figuring out a plan for arranging that space to suit your lifestyle will make the entire decorating process easier.

To lay out a successful room you will need a few tools:

1. A TAPE MEASURE
2. GRAPH PAPER
3. A PENCIL
4. DRAWN-TO-SCALE FURNITURE TEMPLATES (SEE PAGE 193)

Follow this process:

- Start by measuring the space with your tape measure. Make sure you record the correct measurements on a rough sketch of the room.

- Note where windows, doors, lights, electrical outlets, heating vents and other such items are located.

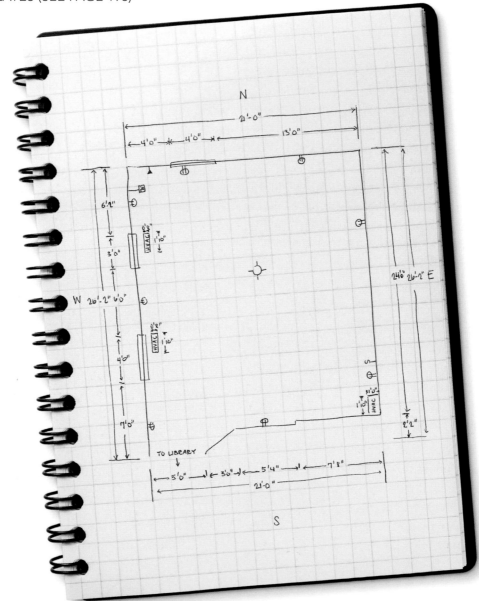

- Once you have finished your rough sketch, transfer the sketch onto graph paper using the squares to draw the room to scale. Typically, one square on graph paper will be equal to one foot. Again, make sure to note the locations of windows, doors, outlets, and so on.

- You can use this finished to-scale drawing to help you figure out the best way to arrange furniture within the space. This is where having furniture templates becomes useful. You can cut out paper shapes to represent each piece of furniture you will need in the space and then arrange them (and rearrange them) on your graph paper drawing of the room until you have an arrangement that works and feels comfortable.

Of course, this plan is not always foolproof. Sometimes a layout that works on paper just doesn't translate well to the actual space. But at the very least, starting with such a plan offers a strong point of reference that you can use as a jumping off place in decorating a room.

COLOR PLANNING

From space planning, we move on to color theory. Color plays a *huge* role in the overall feeling of a house. And honestly, trying to feel at home in a space that is not a reflection of your color preferences never works. So finding the types of colors you are drawn to is of the utmost importance when you are planning out a space.

Try this exercise. Grab a stack of home décor magazines or books (like this one!), or alternately, go online to one of the many décor-related websites that are available. Sift through the photos of rooms and note the rooms that catch your eye. Is there an overall color theme? Is there a different type of theme? Before I meet with clients for the first time, I always ask them to create an inspiration file of this type. I ask them to save numerous photos of rooms that they like.

One time in particular, I remember sorting through the inspiration photos with one of my clients and noticing that every one of them contained bookshelves and the color yellow. When I pointed this out to my client, it surprised her. She hadn't even noticed that all of the rooms contained those two elements. But this is a perfect illustration of what I mean. When you collect images of rooms that you love, a theme often times emerges. And most often, a color palette will predominate in the photos you save.

I love neutral color palettes. My favorite colors are white and gray. I do love pink and navy blue and even orange. And at points in time, I have tried to incorporate more color into the décor of my house, thinking that my neutral palette isn't interesting enough, or that I should like to live in colorful surroundings more than I do. But inevitably, I return to gray and white and cream and linen. That is the palette that makes me the happiest. It is the palette that I am drawn to whenever I look at décor books, magazines, and websites. And because of this, it is the palette in which I feel the most at home, the most calm, peaceful, and nurtured.

DÉCOR STYLE

YOU CAN APPLY this same inspiration concept to help you define the type of decorating style that you favor. The photos you save will necessarily indicate a pattern that will help you to define your style. My client who loved yellow and bookcases didn't even realize how much she was drawn to those things until we analyzed her inspiration photos.

Whether you're drawn to country, cottage, contemporary, or transitional, the images you find appealing will be helpful in determining the sort of look that will accurately reflect the type of home you want to create.

Do not feel, however, that just because you favor a certain type of look, you can only use pieces that are representative of that style. The most successful rooms combine different types of styles to create a comfortable, lived-in look. Even a very traditional space can benefit from a little bit of contemporary décor. And the opposite is also true. A bit of traditional décor brings a sense of history to a more modern interior.

Remember decorating isn't about following a certain set of rules. Rather, I like to think that decorating rules are there simply to define a framework from which we can follow our hearts to create spaces and homes we will love!

FILL IN THE DETAILS

ACCESSORIZING YOUR HOME is like adding the frosting on a cake. If the cake itself isn't delicious, no amount of frosting will be able to make it so. And if the framework of your room design isn't successful, accessories won't be able to save the space. But if you start with a well-designed space and good base pieces, the accessories you add will help to make the space into a masterpiece.

Truthfully, accessorizing can be tricky. And this is where some of the "rules of decorating" can really help in making the space work. In particular, when considering accessories, remember the concepts of scale and repetition. A lot of little accessories will create a sense of clutter, while too many large accessories might overwhelm the space. Rather, aim to mix small and large accessories in inviting groupings. Here's where another one of those

decorating rules come in handy. When creating groupings of accessories make sure to incorporate the Rule of Threes (or more accurately three, five, and seven). Accessories look better grouped in odd numbers.

Also, although symmetry is restful and pleasing, aim to use "approximate symmetry" rather than repeating the same ideas exactly on each side of a mantle, buffet, or room. Approximate symmetry is using objects that balance one another out in scale, color, or texture but that are not identical.

SAFETY FIRST

WHEN DECORATING FOR families, safety is definitely a concern. Following sensible precautions will make your space a safe haven for children as well as adults.

Tips to consider:

- Anchor tall pieces of furniture, art, and mirrors to the wall so that they will not tip over. Bookcases are especially tempting for young ones to climb on. Be cautious that they are not only attached to the wall but also that heavy items are displayed on lower shelves.

- Avoid pieces of furniture with materials that are likely to harm small children. Or alternately, take steps to childproof such furniture pieces. For example, tables with metal tops look great but might not be practical for children who could injure themselves on sharp corners.

- Choose each display item that will be within reach of small children with regard to its size and ability to break.

THIS CHEERFUL AND COZY COTTAGE IS HOME
TO AN ENERGETIC AND HAPPY GAGGLE OF
GIRLS, BUSY PARENTS, AND AN ADORABLE PUP
WHO DEFINITELY HAS THE GOOD LIFE.

CHARMING & CHEERFUL

ENTRY

WHAT DOES THIS SPACE SAY?

Hello! We are a happy, friendly, and busy family who love to laugh. Come in and take your shoes off!

WHAT MAKES THIS SPACE FAMILY FRIENDLY?

This compact entryway is filled with space-saving ideas that make the room function and feel like it is much larger than it is. Taking an under-utilized coat closet and converting it into a built-in mudroom bench and storage helps to create a more usable space for this busy family. Adding a pretty turquoise entry table provides a place to drop mail or set car keys.

The light and bright color scheme works to help the space feel more expansive, and the built-in "furniture" increases the usability of the space within its compact footprint. With three school-aged daughters, easily accessible storage helps to make this space functional for the whole family, and washable fabrics keep the functionality of the space reasonable.

WHAT FEARS NEED TO BE OVERCOME?

The number one concern most people have with open storage like this is that it will begin to look cluttered and ultimately not be an attractive welcome for visitors. This is certainly a possibility. Hanging up coats is not always a priority for young children. Let's face it, it is rarely a priority for young children. As a homeowner, you have to decide whether the ease of open storage balances out your desire for the ability to hide clutter.

WHAT COMPROMISE IS REQUIRED?

The compromise in this space is the fact that it requires upkeep to keep coats, shoes, and backpacks from looking cluttered. The reward is a welcoming and functional space to keep this family organized in their daily comings and goings.

BORROW *these* IDEAS

TURN A LITTLE-USED CLOSET into a mud-bench. By removing the doors and adding a bench with built-in storage as well as some hooks for coats and bags, you add usable square footage to your space. Cheerful pillows and baskets to hide the clutter make the space inviting as well as functional.

CREATE A REVOLVING PHOTO DISPLAY using this simple idea. Craft a frame from thin wood strips and use eye hooks to string twine back and forth across the hooks. Then simply add photos to the twine using clips. The photos can be easily switched out as new ones are added.

LIVING
ROOM

WHAT DOES THIS SPACE SAY?

We are fun-loving, quirky, and adventurous. Family is everything!

WHAT MAKES THIS SPACE FAMILY FRIENDLY?

This living room is purposely devoid of a coffee table. The homeowner felt that the compact space was more livable without one. To make up for the lack of table space, a whimsical gold pouf serves as a makeshift table, extra seating, or a place to put your feet up.

The pretty chairs were a budget-friendly buy, so even though they are light in tone, they are not too precious for everyday use. The white sofa sports a washable slipcover. The colorful gallery wall boasts several similarly toned pictures from a family photo session, and a grand piano sits center stage ready for spur-of-the-moment recitals.

WHAT FEARS NEED TO BE OVERCOME?

The biggest concern for many families is the use of light colors in their décor. This space incorporates a white sofa, a pale area rug, and light-toned chairs as well as white walls and window treatments. As a homeowner, you have to balance your fear of stains versus your desire for a light and bright space.

WHAT COMPROMISE IS REQUIRED?

A good compromise to make when you want to lighten up your upholstered pieces is the use of slipcovers. Fitted slipcovers allow a piece of furniture to have the appearance of upholstery but to be cleaned easily when needed. Opt for washable slipcovers to avoid costly dry cleaning, but realize that you might have to wash the slipcover fairly often depending on how much use the space gets.

BORROW *This* IDEA

GALLERY WALLS ARE A GREAT WAY to display a variety of family photos or artwork in one space. To create a cohesive feel, try using similarly colored frames. Or choose a variety of frames for an eclectic, collected-over-time display.

DINING ROOM

WHAT DOES THIS SPACE SAY?

Hungry? Pull up a chair (or bench) and dig in!

WHAT MAKES THIS SPACE FAMILY FRIENDLY?

The distressed finish on the dining table is a perfect choice for families because it disguises the inevitable scratches and dings that come with everyday use. Incorporating a bench into the seating allows for extra bodies at the table without searching the house for additional chairs.

WHAT FEARS NEED TO BE OVERCOME?

Upholstered seating at the dining table can be nerve-wracking. Rugs beneath tables can have the same concerns attached to them. Spills are a fact of life, regardless of age, although they are definitely more common with the younger set. As a homeowner, you have to balance out your desire for the inviting feel of upholstery and the practicality of wood or metal.

WHAT COMPROMISE IS REQUIRED?

Choosing washable fabrics and rugs, or employing fabric protectants, allow for the use of soft finishes in eating areas. Just realize that there will be days when a little (or a lot) of elbow grease will be required to keep the space looking spotless.

BORROW *These* IDEAS

SHELVES ON THE WALL allow for displays that can be changed out seasonally to keep the room looking fresh and current.

CREATING A CENTERPIECE ON a tray allows it to be easily moved when it is time to eat and then replaced in a snap once meal time is over.

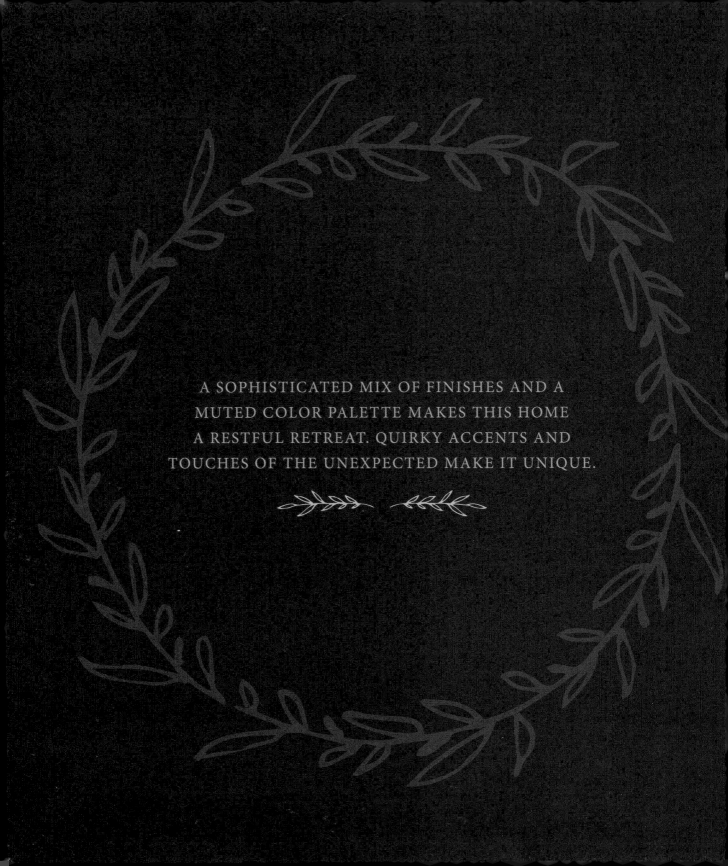

A SOPHISTICATED MIX OF FINISHES AND A
MUTED COLOR PALETTE MAKES THIS HOME
A RESTFUL RETREAT. QUIRKY ACCENTS AND
TOUCHES OF THE UNEXPECTED MAKE IT UNIQUE.

CURATED & CULTIVATED

29

GREAT ROOM

WHAT DOES THIS SPACE SAY?

Just because a space is hardworking doesn't mean it has to look like it is. With two businesses and a musical group, we literally never sit still, but this room keeps up with us beautifully.

WHAT MAKES THIS SPACE FAMILY FRIENDLY?

Multiple seating areas and the incorporation of the family's musical interests into the space make the room perfect for rehearsing, lounging, and socializing. Finishes in this space are a bit more sophisticated since the children are older, but the emphasis on catering to the needs of the family's lifestyle is evident.

WHAT FEARS NEED TO BE OVERCOME?

Many people are drawn to a neutral palette but worry that their home could turn out to be nothing more than a boring beige box. This complex space is proof that neutral and boring are not synonyms.

With pale bleached floors, warm textured walls, layered area rugs, and myriad different finishes, this room is unbelievably interesting. Small pops of turquoise and apricot serve to accent the neutrals beautifully but don't overpower them.

WHAT COMPROMISE IS REQUIRED?

This is the main living space in this house, so it houses the television of course. Electronics are a part of everyday life, but they don't always lend themselves to the look of a room. The family members aren't big television watchers, but they didn't want to do away with the flat screen altogether, so they compromised by leaning a large piece of artwork on the mantle to cover the TV until it is needed.

BORROW *This* IDEA

CREATE A 3-D GALLERY of your favorite family pictures. The photos displayed on this hearth are actually small canvases, but a similar look could be achieved by adhering family photos to wood blocks using decoupage medium. The blocks can then be arranged and rearranged to create an interactive gallery of family photos.

KITCHEN

WHAT DOES THIS SPACE SAY?

The kitchen is definitely the heart of the home. That's why it's in the center of everything. Make yourself at home in our kitchen, and you'll never miss the comings and goings of this family as you enjoy our hospitality.

WHAT MAKES THIS SPACE FAMILY FRIENDLY?

A generous island and a built-in computer desk/hutch make this kitchen perfect for the entire family to be together while eating, conversing, catching up on email, or posting a status update online.

WHAT FEARS NEED TO BE OVERCOME?

Finding a place for a computer station in a kitchen can strike fear into the heart of even the most intrepid designer. How to make a space functional as both a home office and a kitchen can be confusing, but it's certainly not impossible.

WHAT COMPROMISE IS REQUIRED?

A multifunctional work area/storage space such as the one in this kitchen is the perfect compromise between form and function. Open storage houses pretty dishes, even drinks, that fit within the framework of the home's décor. Closed storage houses office essentials and less attractive necessities.

BORROW *This* IDEA

TRY INCORPORATING DIFFERENT TYPES of finishes into a single space. For example, in this kitchen, two different countertops are used: one on the island and one on the perimeter cabinetry. If you're not in the market for a kitchen remodel at the moment, try adopting this same strategy in other areas of your home. Don't be afraid to combine colors and even patterns to add interest.

GATHERING SPACE

WHAT DOES THIS SPACE SAY?

Awkward spaces can add interest and beauty to a home as easily as any other room. Sit down and read a bit or stop to reflect on the day.

WHAT MAKES THIS SPACE FAMILY FRIENDLY?

This corner of the house is unique and intriguing. A small built-in bench adds interest to an otherwise predictable hallway. Family photos tacked to a mounted wood board make it a place for memories. The bedroom just off this hallway is a memorial to the eldest daughter in the family who was lost too soon. A pretty pink guitar is a makeshift bulletin board covered with notes of love and support from friends. Just outside the bedroom and across from the bench, a pretty spiral staircase rounds its way downstairs. Unique built-in shelves provide display space for mementos and art important to the family.

WHAT FEARS NEED TO BE OVERCOME?

Some people fear adding sentimentality to a space. But, in truth, what else is a home if not a sanctuary for its inhabitants? Photos, artwork, notes, and mementos are all important ways to bind a family together and create a sense of belonging.

WHAT COMPROMISE IS REQUIRED?

Dedicating space to family memories within a home is not a compromise. Rather, it is a necessity. Make sure to carve out space in your home to create a strong sense of family unity.

BORROW *This* IDEA

OFTENTIMES PEOPLE GET CAUGHT up in the idea that art needs to be framed in order to be displayed. This family photo gallery is a perfect example of how a casual display can be just as effective. Push pins are used to tack unframed portraits to a board. Try this in your own home to create a casual, welcoming vibe.

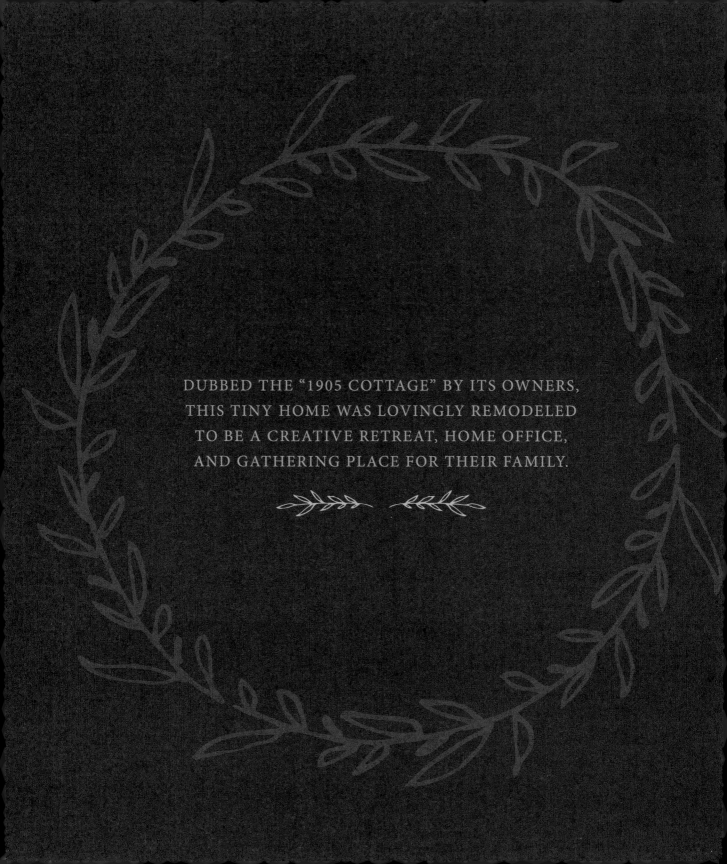

DUBBED THE "1905 COTTAGE" BY ITS OWNERS,
THIS TINY HOME WAS LOVINGLY REMODELED
TO BE A CREATIVE RETREAT, HOME OFFICE,
AND GATHERING PLACE FOR THEIR FAMILY.

COZY & COMFORTABLE

KITCHEN

WHAT DOES THIS SPACE SAY?

This little kitchen is the heart of the home. Come on in and grab a bite to eat or just sit and chat. We love visitors!

WHAT MAKES THIS SPACE FAMILY FRIENDLY?

Loads of pretty white cabinetry provides oodles of storage for this family of six. The pretty table-turned-center-island provides a central gathering spot to sit, to eat, or to simply shoot the breeze. Faux succulents give the look and feel of live greenery without the maintenance. Metal barstools weather the wear and tear of family life easily while graphic patterns and citrus-hued accessories give the space a contemporary punch. Modern conveniences combined with vintage charm make the space the true heart of this little cottage.

WHAT FEARS NEED TO BE OVERCOME?

Marble countertops are undeniably beautiful and add a great deal of character to this white-on-white space. But they are also high maintenance. The double fears of etching and staining give many homeowners pause when considering marble for kitchen use.

WHAT COMPROMISE IS REQUIRED?

When opting to use marble countertops in any space, homeowners need to be ready and willing to deal with the patina that comes from daily use. Marble is certainly not a carefree choice for countertops, but its beauty is worth the compromise.

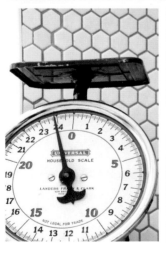

BORROW *these* IDEAS

OPTING TO USE A TABLE for a kitchen island is a great idea for families. The table can be moved when extra floor space is needed or even changed out when a new look is wanted.

THE CHEERY YELLOW CHANDELIER in this kitchen was found at a thrift store and given new life with a few coats of spray paint. To achieve this look in your home, scour flea markets, thrift stores, and yard sales for a chandelier with great lines and an outdated finish. After thoroughly cleaning the piece, spray it with a coat of primer and follow up with several coats of spray paint in the color of your choice.

BATHROOM

WHAT DOES THIS SPACE SAY?

This bath might be small, but it is hardworking!

WHAT MAKES THIS SPACE FAMILY FRIENDLY?

The choice of an open vanity provides easy-to-reach storage for towels and washcloths. The baskets hide less attractive essentials while still keeping them handy. Floor to ceiling tile makes for easy cleaning of walls and a row of hooks keeps the pretty coral hand towels readily accessible while energizing the space with a dose of color.

WHAT FEARS NEED TO BE OVERCOME?

Open storage can be a blessing and a curse. It allows family members—and guests—to find what they need easily, but it can also become an unsightly mess in a hurry.

WHAT COMPROMISE IS REQUIRED?

If you are going to use open storage in any space, realize that you will be required to keep it organized and clutter-free in order to maintain an attractive look. Time will be the big compromise in this case, but you can save money by making your everyday essentials a part of your décor.

BORROW *this* IDEA

PAINT DIPPED VASES ARE an easy and fun way to update a space. To create a similar masterpiece, first choose a vase. It doesn't have to be wood; glass vases work just as well. Use painter's tape to protect the part of the vase you want to leave unpainted, and to give a crisp clean "dip" line. Then cover the bottom part of the vase with several coats of craft paint in a color of your choice. Once the paint dries, remove the painter's tape and add flowers for a cute and current display.

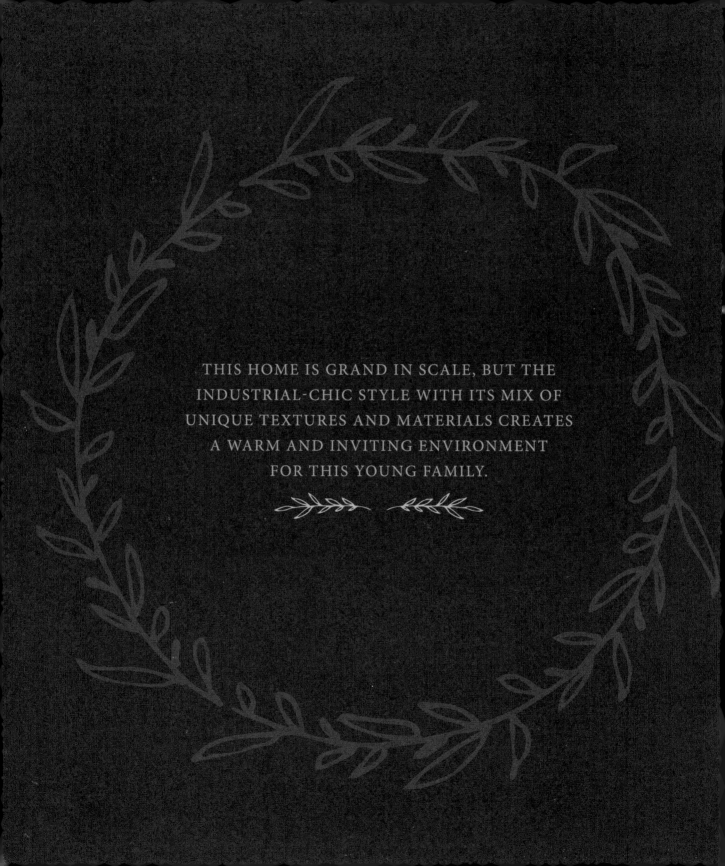

THIS HOME IS GRAND IN SCALE, BUT THE
INDUSTRIAL-CHIC STYLE WITH ITS MIX OF
UNIQUE TEXTURES AND MATERIALS CREATES
A WARM AND INVITING ENVIRONMENT
FOR THIS YOUNG FAMILY.

COOL & CURRENT

GREAT ROOM

65

WHAT DOES THIS SPACE SAY?

As a family with rough and tumble boys, we rarely sit still, but we sure do like to spend time together! Come on in and join the fun!

WHAT MAKES THIS SPACE FAMILY FRIENDLY?

The darker colors in this home's palette and the easy-to-clean leather sofa make this space perfect for a family of small boys. Choosing a sectional allows for lots of seating or makes a great lounging spot to catch the big game on the TV. One of the big dilemmas homeowners face in decorating multifunctional great rooms like this is where to place the television set. Opting to put the TV on a low console rather than mounting it on the wall makes it easy to view while sitting on the sofa and provides simple cord-hiding options. The brick focal wall behind the TV is intentionally left unadorned to focus on the texture of the wall and allow television viewing with few distractions.

WHAT FEARS NEED TO BE OVERCOME?

The use of cowhide rugs can be intimidating for homeowners who have small children or who entertain often. Fear of how to care for them and whether or not stains can be removed keep some homeowners from investing in these natural beauties.

WHAT COMPROMISE IS REQUIRED?

Interestingly, there isn't much compromise when it comes to adding cowhide rugs to a space. They require a bit of mainte-nance (like occasionally brushing the fur on the rug), but stains are actually fairly easy to remove with a damp cloth and diluted soap water. A bit of white vinegar and water can also remove less-than-pleasant smells from these types of rugs. ("Cowhide Cleaning and Curling" *Gorgeous Creatures*, July 17, 2014, http://www.gorgeouscreatures.co.nz/About+Cowhide+Rugs/Cowhide+Cleaning+and+Curling.html.)

BORROW *This* IDEA

TERRARIUMS ARE FABULOUS AS décor and offer a bit of a science lesson on the side! To make a terrarium like this one simply find a large glass bowl—a fish bowl is ideal. Start with a layer of one to two inches of activated charcoal on the bottom of the container. Mix more charcoal with potting soil and add it to the bowl. Add hardy plants such as succulents and top remaining exposed soil with a layer of moss. Make sure to water the plants initially, but not too often after that to prevent root rot. (Katie A. Ketelsen, "Terrariums: A Guide to Plants and Care," *Better Homes and Gardens*, accessed July 17, 2104, http://www.bhg.com/gardening/houseplants/care/make-a-terrarium/#page=1.)

LOFT
PLAY SPACE

WHAT DOES THIS SPACE SAY?

Creativity is important to us! Let's have some fun using our imaginations, without all our techy toys.

WHAT MAKES THIS SPACE FAMILY FRIENDLY?

Besides the obvious fact that this is a play space, this room lends itself well to family life because of its casual feel and lack of pretension. A fun canvas tent keeps with the industrial-chic feeling of the house, and accompanied by faux trees, it encourages pretend play. An entire wall coated in chalkboard paint allows budding Picassos to draw to their hearts' content. Adding a touch of whimsy to a home is always a good thing. Homes that don't take themselves too seriously are always the most comfortable.

WHAT FEARS NEED TO BE OVERCOME?

There can be a certain amount of trepidation involved with the idea of devoting a centrally located space—such as this open loft—entirely to children.

WHAT COMPROMISE IS REQUIRED?

Giving up space that could be used for other activities is always a compromise. That said, granting children a place to call their own can oftentimes discourage the use of the entire house as a play area.

BORROW *this* IDEA

CREATE A CHALKBOARD WALL. Creating a chalkboard wall is easier than you might think. There are a number of ways to tackle it. Commercial chalkboard paints are now available in a variety of colors. Or, if you prefer a custom color, you can create your own chalkboard paint by adding sanded grout to matte latex paint. You can also try chalkboard medium—a clear craft paint that turns just about any surface into a chalkboard by simply painting over it. Just make sure to let your chalkboard cure for seventy-two hours, and then season it by rubbing the side of a piece of chalk over the entire surface and wiping it off before writing on it for the first time.

STOP
LISTEN
LOOK

BIG BOYS'
BEDROOM

1 4

2 5

3 6

WHAT DOES THIS SPACE SAY?

A comfy bedroom is the ultimate space to nap and relax. Snuggle in and get cozy.

WHAT MAKES THIS SPACE FAMILY FRIENDLY?

Warm woods and washable duvet covers make these beds perfect for boys with a penchant for play. Cozy down comforters and pillows make them comfortable enough to lull those same energetic boys to sleep. Fun touches like train-inspired sconces and locker-style storage make this a little boy's paradise.

WHAT FEARS NEED TO BE OVERCOME?

Many homeowners are afraid of making bedrooms too reflective of a child's age, fearing that this will cause them to have to redecorate too quickly.

WHAT COMPROMISE IS REQUIRED?

Choosing fabric patterns that are timeless will allow the space to grow with its occupants. Age-specific décor is best limited to accessories and art which can easily and inexpensively be changed as children grow. In this space, the train-themed art, lighting, and pillows let visitors know it belongs to little boys—while classic beds, linens, and curtains can easily last into the preteen years.

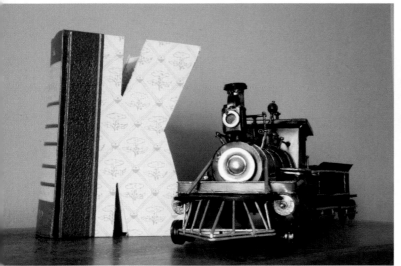

BORROW *These* IDEAS

CAN'T FIND (OR AFFORD) the perfect bed? DIY it! These beds were made by the homeowners using plans they found online.

CREATE BOOK LETTERS. THESE letters are made using old decorative books that can easily be found at your local thrift store. Take the book and sketch out the letter you wish to make. Ideally letters should be the same size as the book and must include the binding for this project to work. Then, using a jigsaw or a scroll saw, simply cut along the lines you have sketched to create the letter. To display, fan the book out a bit and set it on a table top or bookcase.

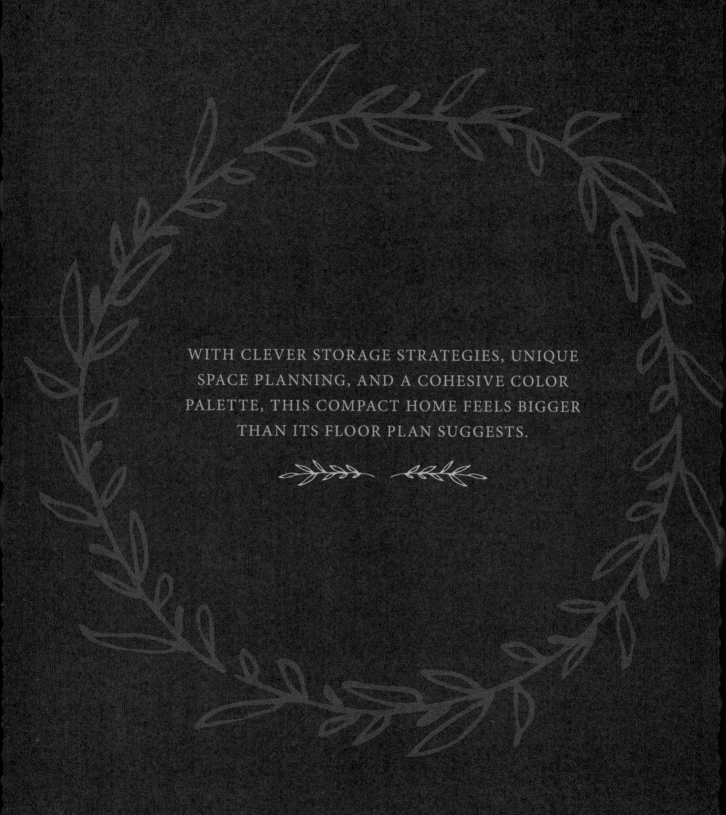

WITH CLEVER STORAGE STRATEGIES, UNIQUE
SPACE PLANNING, AND A COHESIVE COLOR
PALETTE, THIS COMPACT HOME FEELS BIGGER
THAN ITS FLOOR PLAN SUGGESTS.

PETITE & PRETTY

READING NOOK

WHAT DOES THIS SPACE SAY?

Climb on up and settle in with a good book. There's nothing better than a pile of comfy pillows and a great page-turner!

WHAT MAKES THIS SPACE FAMILY FRIENDLY?

This loft-turned-reading-nook is a clever way to convert an awkward space into a room the entire family can enjoy. The bed was made to look like a built-in, although it can be moved out of the space should it ever need to be. With hidden drawer storage underneath, bookshelves full of books, and clever curtains that can be used for privacy, this space is a retreat for a busy family in search of a little R & R.

WHAT FEARS NEED TO BE OVERCOME?

Built-in furniture can be a source of anxiety for homeowners because of the commitment to a particular look. But in a home where space is at a premium, built-ins are a clever solution to optimize the usefulness of what otherwise might be under-utilized real estate.

WHAT COMPROMISE IS REQUIRED?

In this space, the look—and space-saving usefulness—of built-in furniture was accomplished by creating a daybed that appears to be built in but is actually removable. This is a clever tactic that can be used in many different ways. It is possible to construct bookcases that appear to be built in by adding crown molding to store-bought pieces. Or try building a banquette that has the appearance of a built-in by modifying store-bought benches to fit in a tight kitchen corner. With a little bit of creativity and out-of-the-box thinking, this concept can be a lifesaver in a compact space.

BORROW *These* IDEAS

CREATE YOUR OWN COLOR-GRADATION artwork by purchasing small six-by-six-inch preprimed canvases at your local art or craft store. Paint the first canvas the color of your choice at its full intensity. For the next canvas, add some white to the full-intensity color and paint it on. Continue adding a bit of white to lighten the paint color as you paint each canvas. Strive to have the lightened color reach almost white by the time you reach the final canvas. Once the canvases are dry, you can hang them up in order, or mix them up to create a tonal masterpiece!

TRY CREATING AN ART piece out of scrap wood. Scraps of wood cut to the same width but different lengths and thicknesses create a stunning 3-D art piece. To make a similar piece, attach scrap wood to a backing board—plywood works well—using wood glue. Play with the order of the pieces to create different depths. The scraps used in this piece were naturally different colors, but if you are using wood that is all the same species, consider staining or even painting the pieces before you attach them to give the piece some additional interest.

KENNEBUNKPORT
ST GEORGE
BOSTON
PLYMOUTH
ALM DESERT
EW YORK
RTLAND ME
NIAGARA FALLS
NEWPORT
WASHINGTON DC
OLD ORCHARD

DINING ROOM

91

91

WHAT DOES THIS SPACE SAY?

Gather around the table for good food and friendly conversation. The more the merrier.

WHAT MAKES THIS SPACE FAMILY FRIENDLY?

A table with generous proportions and an easy-care finish makes this an ideal dining space for a family with four growing children. The addition of a vintage buffet provides plenty of entertaining space when guests join in. With the room's proximity to the kitchen and living areas, and its ample workspace, it is the perfect spot for art projects and homework in this open-concept home.

WHAT FEARS NEED TO BE OVERCOME?

Homeowners traditionally shy away from the idea of using larger pieces of furniture in smaller homes. But this doesn't always need to be the case. The dining table in this space measures a whopping seven feet long and nearly four feet wide.

WHAT COMPROMISE IS REQUIRED?

The main compromise that needs to be made in a space such as this is merely a willingness to break the rules of scale. Large pieces can absolutely be used in smaller homes. And in the case of this family, a large dining table was an absolute necessity. And despite the fact that the table is big, it doesn't overpower the space.

When choosing larger pieces of furniture for smaller spaces, follow a couple of simple rules. First, opt for pieces that allow light to show through. Note the open feeling of the legs on the table. They are not big and heavy but rather open and airy, allowing the piece to feel light despite its larger measurements. Second, choose a single large piece of furniture per room. If you are trying to cram a small space full with many large pieces the space will simply feel smaller. But adding a single large piece often times has the opposite effect, allowing the space to feel roomier than it actually is.

Charlotte

BORROW *These* IDEAS

GIVE A DINING ROOM a sense of history by choosing a vintage buffet to use as a sideboard. The buffet in this room has seen a few reincarnations with different paint colors, its current version being white. Consider painting a buffet a trendy color for a burst of the unexpected.

THESE CLEVER COASTERS are simply quartz countertop samples. Visit stone suppliers or design showrooms to see if they have samples that they no longer need.

CLEVER PLACE CARDS WERE never simpler to make than these. Cut paper into small one-by-two-inch pieces and write each guest's name in a pretty script on the paper. For more interest, try using metallic or colorful markers. Then simply nestle the paper into the prongs of a fork.

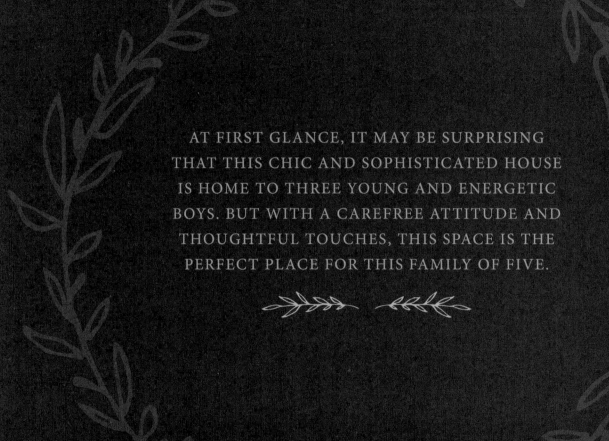

AT FIRST GLANCE, IT MAY BE SURPRISING
THAT THIS CHIC AND SOPHISTICATED HOUSE
IS HOME TO THREE YOUNG AND ENERGETIC
BOYS. BUT WITH A CAREFREE ATTITUDE AND
THOUGHTFUL TOUCHES, THIS SPACE IS THE
PERFECT PLACE FOR THIS FAMILY OF FIVE.

LUXE & LIVABLE

FAMILY ROOM

WHAT DOES THIS SPACE SAY?

We are a well-traveled and interesting bunch! But we sure know how to kick back and have a good time. Come on in and join the fun!

WHAT MAKES THIS SPACE FAMILY FRIENDLY?

The appeal of this space is that it looks as if it were torn right out of the pages of a decorating magazine. At first glance, it does not look like your typical family home. But look closer. Distressed brown leather Chesterfield-style sofas are perfect for rough and tumble boys. An oversize (and furry) beanbag chair invites lounging and encourages family members to kick back and watch the latest movie. Wood pieces with purposely aged patinas aren't too precious for children to use as play tables, and the oversize coffee table invites family and friends to gather round for entertainment.

WHAT FEARS NEED TO BE OVERCOME?

Having higher quality items in a living space with little children is probably one of the single largest concerns for most parents. And there is not an easy solution, but this house is proof that it can be done successfully.

WHAT COMPROMISE IS REQUIRED?

This house epitomizes my philosophy of living with items you love rather than waiting for your children to be grown and moved out of the house. More fragile items are placed on the perimeter of the room, allowing for their visual appeal but removing them from the main gathering space of the room. The finishes of the pieces that highlight the space are family friendly and easily cared for. The big compromise in a space such as this is realizing that despite the careful placement of some of the more fragile pieces of décor, they still might become casualties of a stray ball or another flying object. (Let's face it. This is a house with little boys.) Realizing that things are just things is the biggest compromise any homeowner needs to make. And placing easy-care finishes, such as leather, on the main pieces of furniture allows for the style to take center stage without worrying about possible spills.

BORROW *this* IDEA

GIVE NEW LIFE TO dated fabric chairs by painting them! To paint fabric without making it "crunchy" and uncomfortable, purchase fabric medium and add it to your paint of choice. In the case of these chairs, chalk paint was used. Brush the paint and fabric medium mixture right onto the fabric and allow it to cure and dry thoroughly for several days before moving it into the living space.

BOYS' BEDROOM

WHAT DOES THIS SPACE SAY?

Creativity is king in this house! Come imagine and dream in this unique and comfy bedroom. Adventures await during waking hours or in your dreams!

WHAT MAKES THIS SPACE FAMILY FRIENDLY?

The boys' bedroom is comfy and cozy with duvet covers that can easily be removed and washed in case of a mishap. Child size furnishings bring everything down to scale for these smaller members of the family. The addition of the Australian flag—a nod to their mother's home country—family photos, and artwork painted by their mother bring the boys a sense of history and belonging and reinforces the fact that family comes first.

WHAT FEARS NEED TO BE OVERCOME?

The use of nontraditional headboards in this room is a bold choice and one that the homeowner took seriously. They were originally added on a trial basis, but the boys love them and they add such character to the space that they have remained.

WHAT COMPROMISE IS REQUIRED?

Compromise isn't exactly the right word to use for this space. Rather, a sense of careful planning. Using mirrors for headboards has worked out for this family because the headboards are securely anchored to the wall, and roughhousing on the beds isn't common. Instead, the bedroom is a place for quiet play in this house. Rough and tumble action takes place in the playroom. Defining specific and appropriate uses for particular rooms is a great way for families to bring in the sorts of décor they want while providing an outlet for natural childhood behavior.

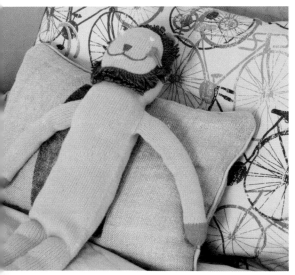

BORROW *These* IDEAS

GIVE AN OLD SCHOOL chair new life. Pieces of sturdy leather were cut into squares and glued patchwork style to this little chair to give it a one-of-a-kind look that keeps with the home's aesthetic.

CREATE A MINI-ART GALLERY for your children. Place a painted wood backing into an oversize frame. Then hang minicanvases or other pieces of your children's artwork from small nails or hooks. This is a perfect way to create a rotating display of your children's latest masterpieces!

MASTER
BEDROOM

WHAT DOES THIS SPACE SAY?

Relaxation is my specialty. Come in and unwind after a busy day. Sweet dreams are waiting.

WHAT MAKES THIS SPACE FAMILY FRIENDLY?

This master bedroom is truly a sanctuary for these busy parents of three. But as all parents know, when children are little, Mom and Dad's room has to serve the entire family well. A king-size upholstered bed assures that the whole family can snuggle up together when needed. And the addition of a baby hammock for the family's tiniest member means that his parents can get the rest they need but still have him close by when he needs attention in the wee hours of the morning.

WHAT FEARS NEED TO BE OVERCOME?

Parents of new babies are oftentimes concerned with how to keep baby close at hand without adding unattractive plastic pieces or bulky cribs that don't quite fit in the master bedroom. Finding the best way to make life livable for everyone during those first few months can be a conundrum.

WHAT COMPROMISE IS REQUIRED?

Picking a newborn bed that doesn't overpower the adult space in your home is possible. You can find one that is both practical and beautiful. In the case of these homeowners, they've turned to the addition of a baby hammock that blends in perfectly with their neutral décor and is practical for their lifestyle as well. Bassinets and cradles are currently available in a number of styles that can look both sophisticated and chic, allowing parents to maintain the restful atmosphere of their master retreat while still providing for the needs of their new little addition.

BORROW *This* IDEA

CREATE EASY BURLAP MONOGRAM pillows. Using a computer and printer, print out a large, uppercase letter of your choice using a simple font. Cut it out and use it as a template for creating your monogram. Trace the outline of the monogram onto your burlap with a pencil, and then fill it in using fabric paint pens or markers. Once the monogram dries, cut the monogram and another piece of burlap into rectangles and stitch them with right sides together. Make sure to leave one corner open so that the pillow can be turned right side out. Once it is right side out, stuff the pillow with cotton batting, and finish stitching the open corner closed.

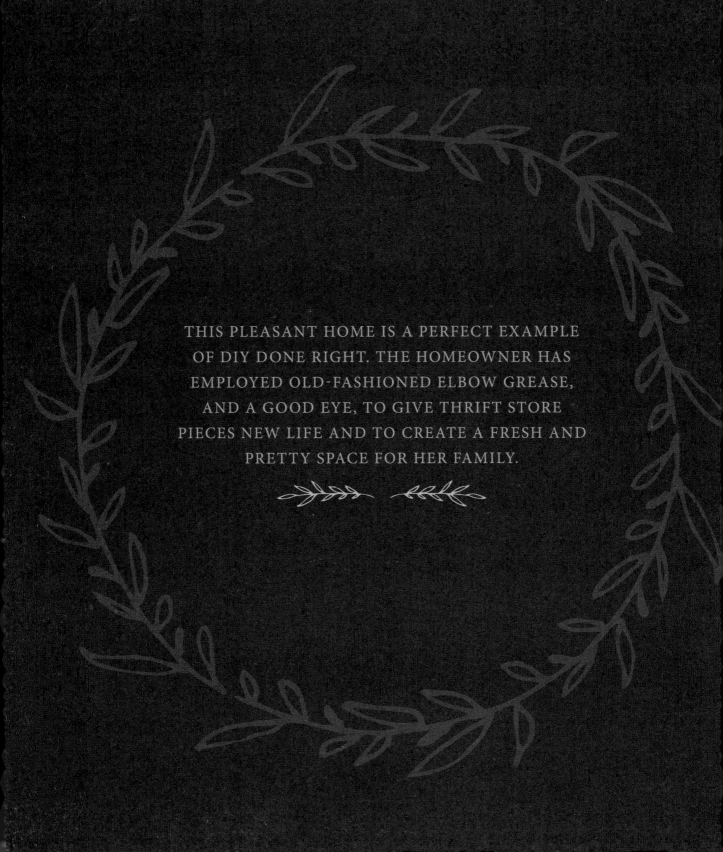

THIS PLEASANT HOME IS A PERFECT EXAMPLE
OF DIY DONE RIGHT. THE HOMEOWNER HAS
EMPLOYED OLD-FASHIONED ELBOW GREASE,
AND A GOOD EYE, TO GIVE THRIFT STORE
PIECES NEW LIFE AND TO CREATE A FRESH AND
PRETTY SPACE FOR HER FAMILY.

BRIGHT & BEACHY

FAMILY ROOM

WHAT DOES THIS SPACE SAY?

Daydream of warm days and sandy beaches. Our family is as open and friendly as sunny skies on the seashore.

WHAT MAKES THIS SPACE FAMILY FRIENDLY?

Space planning can always be challenging, and with an angular configuration, this room could have been quite a challenge. The open placement of the furniture, however, allows for conversation—and even play—in this fresh and colorful family room. Durable finishes such as leather are a perfect choice for a main living area like this one, while painted wood pieces can be freshened up easily if they get chipped.

WHAT FEARS NEED TO BE OVERCOME?

The use of dark leather in a space is always attractive to parents for the ease of care that it provides. The major concern with this same finish is how to make a space look light and bright when the major pieces of furniture are dark.

WHAT COMPROMISE IS REQUIRED?

Using lighter pieces to compensate for the dark hue of the sofas in this room allows the space to maintain its beachy feel. Bright accessories and pops of color help to further the feeling. Combining finishes that require a bit more care with child-friendly materials such as leather allows a room to have depth and interest while still catering to the needs of different-aged family members. Refinishing thrift-store and tag-sale pieces is a wonderful way to create the perfect piece for a room while not investing large amounts of money.

BORROW *This* IDEA

CREATE YOUR OWN SEASCAPE artwork. An abstract seascape is a good way to try your hand at painting. Start with a small, inexpensive canvas for your first foray into painting. Craft paint is also a good starter tool for would-be painters. Several shades of blues and greens as well as a little yellow and pink for the sky should do the trick. Use a bit of water to thin the paint and start at the bottom of the canvas, painting large stripes of blue. Graduate the intensity of the colors and blend with more water until you have a smooth, "liquid" looking finish. To add the sky, use a similar technique with the pink and yellow colors. Leaving a bit of white will give the sky a cloudy appearance. Once you feel confident with your skills you can venture into painting a larger scale canvas like the one in this family room.

DINING ROOM

WHAT DOES THIS SPACE SAY?

Dining is an important family affair. Sit down and enjoy a meal filled with good food and even better conversation.

WHAT MAKES THIS SPACE FAMILY FRIENDLY?

True to the other spaces in this house, the furniture in this cheerful dining room has been given a fresh, new life. Repurposed family pieces, as well as a dining table found for a steal, create a harmonious space full of vintage flavor and ready to serve this family well.

WHAT FEARS NEED TO BE OVERCOME?

The biggest fear most people face when it comes to refinishing furniture is the fear of painting over "good wood." Many people fear that they will ruin a piece of furniture if they take a paint brush to it.

WHAT COMPROMISE IS REQUIRED?

The only compromise required when refinishing pieces of older furniture is being able to stand the critical tone of those who disapprove of painting versus restoring. Ultimately, your home needs to be a reflection of you and your family. It needs to be a place that you love and want to spend time in. If that means painting an older piece of furniture, then by all means, do so.

BORROW *This* IDEA

CREATE DINING ROOM DISPLAY space with mismatched furniture pieces. An old cabinet passed down from family members and a stray shelf painted in matching finishes pair up to make a sweet vintage-style hutch to house pretty bowls, plates, and accessories in this dining room. Just because two furniture pieces didn't come as a set doesn't mean they can't work together to create the perfect look in a room.

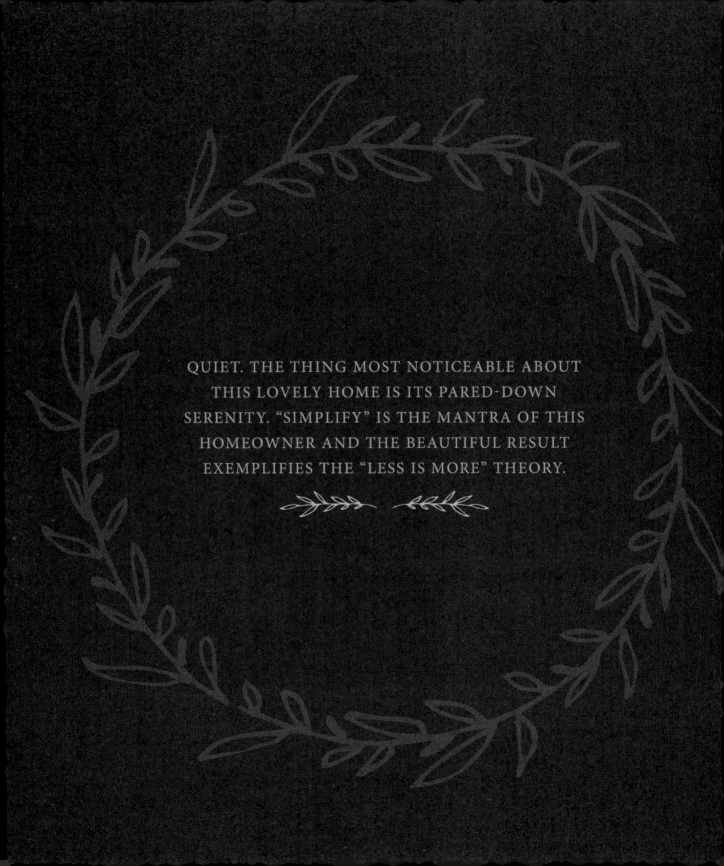

QUIET. THE THING MOST NOTICEABLE ABOUT
THIS LOVELY HOME IS ITS PARED-DOWN
SERENITY. "SIMPLIFY" IS THE MANTRA OF THIS
HOMEOWNER AND THE BEAUTIFUL RESULT
EXEMPLIFIES THE "LESS IS MORE" THEORY.

SIMPLE & SERENE

FAMILY
ROOM

WHAT DOES THIS SPACE SAY?

Curl up on the sofa and enjoy the sun streaming in the windows. Peace and quiet are the rule of the day!

WHAT MAKES THIS SPACE FAMILY FRIENDLY?

The bright and cheerful family room is the center and hub of this home's activity. Hours are spent reading, watching television, or enjoying one another's company. The open space plan allows this family of six to gather without feeling cramped. And the ease of cleaning slipcovered furniture provides peace of mind despite the all-white color scheme. Thoughtfully chosen accessories—which are composed predominantly of family photographs taken by the homeowner—illustrate that family is of the utmost importance.

WHAT FEARS NEED TO BE OVERCOME?

Too often we overdecorate in fear of our homes feeling sterile. But many times too much is just that. Fewer, but thoughtfully chosen, accessories are often more effective and give rooms a more intentional feeling than accessories added for the sake of filling display space.

WHAT COMPROMISE IS REQUIRED?

The ability to leave a space purposely less decorated is intimidating but can have beautiful results. Let the architecture of the room speak, and allow the space to breathe. Unadorned windows let nature take center stage as artwork and bring in natural light that warms the atmosphere of a room. Instead of asking yourself what can be added to a space, figure out what can be removed. It's a different way of wrapping your head around the decorating process, but it might just be what you and your family need.

BORROW *This* IDEA

DISPLAY EMPTY FRAMES AS artwork. To some this might seem counterintuitive. But try choosing frames for their shape or interesting pattern. Paint them all one color or choose frames whose natural finishes work well together. Hang them on a wall to add architectural interest, or prop them on a fireplace mantle or even against the wall on a table for a bit of added depth.

HOME OFFICE

WHAT DOES THIS SPACE SAY?

Let your creative juices flow! Surrounded by things that inspire—a favorite scripture, a pretty collection—this space is meant for work of the imaginative kind.

WHAT MAKES THIS SPACE FAMILY FRIENDLY?

This space allows creativity to flow because of its lovely uncluttered aesthetic. There is plenty of breathing space and room for brainstorming in this light and bright home office. In the same way as the family room, furniture is minimal but carefully chosen to reflect simplicity and comfort. An overstuffed chair swathed in a white cotton slipcover begs the home's inhabitants to sit and visit with whomever is hard at work at the desk.

WHAT FEARS NEED TO BE OVERCOME?

A palette whose predominant color is white can be scary to many people. Many homeowners worry that white will make a space feel sterile or cold. As this space proves, that can be anything but true.

WHAT COMPROMISE IS REQUIRED?

Wood flooring and furniture pieces warm up the mostly white color scheme. When creating a white color scheme it is important to add in texture and natural hues in the form of wood pieces, woven fiber rugs, or baskets. This will enhance the white and make it livable.

BORROW *this* IDEA

ADD A COLLECTION. One of the best ways to bring your family's personality to a space is to add a collection. For maximum impact, display the collection as a whole in one room rather than spreading it around the house. A collection of mercury glass is gathered together on a side table in this home office, creating a focal point and conversation starter that speaks to the interests of the home's inhabitants.

THIS BEAUTIFUL HOME WAS DESIGNED AND
BUILT BY THE HOMEOWNERS THEMSELVES,
GIVING THEM THE RARE LUXURY OF A SPACE
THAT IS EXACTLY CATERED TO THEIR NEEDS.
WITH THREE CHILDREN—TWO GIRLS AND A BOY—
ONE OF THEIR WISH-LIST ITEMS WAS SEPARATE
BATHROOMS. THE RESULTS WERE AMAZING.

FRESH & FABULOUS

GIRLS'
BATHROOM

WHAT DOES THIS SPACE SAY?

It's all in the details. Want to feel beautiful everyday? Start in a space that makes you feel like a princess.

WHAT MAKES THIS SPACE FAMILY FRIENDLY?

When you start your day in a space this lovely, you can't help but smile. The thing that makes this space family friendly is the very fact that it is catered specifically to the two young women who share it. A dual vanity means no jostling for sink or counter space. And pretty-as-a-princess details make a girl feel special.

WHAT FEARS NEED TO BE OVERCOME?

When decorating specifically for the younger members of our families, the types of finishes chosen can always be an area of concern. But just because a space is designed for children doesn't mean attractive features can't be used.

WHAT COMPROMISE IS REQUIRED?

In this case, the homeowners used high-end finishes that they were able to find for pennies on the dollar. Remnant granite makes beautiful countertops for a fraction of the cost. Faucets sourced online provide a custom look without spending a fortune.

BORROW *These* IDEAS

CUSTOMIZE YOUR ARTWORK. Give your family a personalized message by printing out a phrase of your choice in a pale font on thick paper. Then, using an adhesive pen, trace over the words. Cover the adhesive with embossing powder, and use a heat gun to give the wording a 3-D or metallic effect. Follow the instructions on the embossing powder container for specific details. Once the words cool and set, place your paper in a pretty frame and your custom artwork is ready to hang.

HANG MIRRORS OVER MIRRORS. Large plate glass mirrors are a bathroom staple. And let's face it. They're very practical. They are not, however, always the most attractive feature of a space. Try using this clever idea to customize a plate glass mirror. Find small and relatively lightweight decorative mirrors and hang them right over top of the plate glass mirror using outdoor-strength adhesive hooks.

BOY'S
BATHROOM

WHAT DOES THIS SPACE SAY?

I am one hundred percent little boy. But that doesn't mean I have to be covered in dirt. This bathroom is just for me . . . so I guess it's time to clean up!

WHAT MAKES THIS SPACE FAMILY FRIENDLY?

Having the luxury of separate bathrooms for separate genders isn't something most homeowners enjoy. But when you're presented with such an opportunity, embrace it. This bathroom is a masculine mix of colors, textures, and unique touches that help make cleaning up a fun experience for a busy little guy. If you have a child who truly dislikes taking showers—and that's most of them—try adding something fun like these homeowners did. An LED showerhead that changes color makes showering a treat!

WHAT FEARS NEED TO BE OVERCOME?

Dark finishes don't necessarily equal a dark room. Montauk black slate floors and black granite countertops add masculinity to the bathroom but don't make it feel like a cave.

WHAT COMPROMISE IS REQUIRED?

Try using a wall color that is a tint of the darker colored finishes in the space. In this bathroom, gray walls balance out the dark floors and countertops while serving to lighten up the room. Touches of brown in the vanity, the shower curtains, and the artwork add warmth to what otherwise might become a cool-toned space.

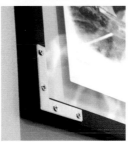

BORROW *This* IDEA

CREATE A 3-D CORK BOARD. Start by cutting a piece of MDF into the shape of your choice with a jigsaw. Then cut a thin sheet of corkboard to the same shape and attach it with spray adhesive. To create the 3-D effect, cut graduated sizes of cork and attach them one on top of the other with spray adhesive. You'll have a one-of-a-kind piece of functional art in no time!

ECLECTIC AND ARTISTIC ARE TWO WORDS THAT
DEFINE NOT ONLY THIS HOME BUT THE FAMILY
THAT LIVES IN IT AS WELL. GEOMETRIC AND ETHNIC
PATTERNS COMBINE WITH A SOPHISTICATED
COLOR PALETTE TO CREATE A HOME THAT IS AS
INTERESTING AS IT IS COMFORTABLE.

GLOBAL & GLAM

159

FAMILY
ROOM

WHAT DOES THIS SPACE SAY?

We are a colorful and well-traveled family with a young and carefree spirit. Come on in and join the fun!

WHAT MAKES THIS SPACE FAMILY FRIENDLY?

Home to a growing young family, the high-low nature of this family room makes it ideal for homeowners who want a current look but don't want to invest their life savings to get it. Combining white Barcelona chairs found online for a deal with clean-lined pieces from IKEA, this room has a high-end and carefully curated appearance without breaking the bank.

WHAT FEARS NEED TO BE OVERCOME?

White fur is a very bold choice with young children in the family. White fur on the floor can be terrifying. But incorporating such a finish within carefully thought out parameters makes it a valid possibility.

WHAT COMPROMISE IS REQUIRED?

There are many finishes that are challenging to use with children. Those which are difficult to clean present the biggest challenge. Smart placement of such items allows them to be used more easily. For example, a white fur area rug is central to the feeling of this space, but using a large scale fur that covers the majority of the space would have been a logistical nightmare. Layering a small rug over a large, easier-to-care-for sisal and underneath a similar-sized coffee table gives the room the texture and interest desired while protecting it at the same time.

BORROW *This* IDEA

PAINT AN ACCENT WALL. Accent walls involving stripes or chevron like this one are easier to achieve than you might think. They involve a bit of math and a lot of taping, but they aren't difficult. Start by laying out your pattern based on the measurements of the wall. Tape off the pattern using painters tape. Seal the edges of the tape to prevent paint from leaking underneath by painting along the edges with the same color as the base coat. After that dries, paint the contrasting color on. Allow to dry, and then remove the painter's tape. Using tonal colors like the gray on gray used here allow a bold pattern to be incorporated without overpowering a space.

POWDER
ROOM

WHAT DOES THIS SPACE SAY?

Even tiny spaces deserve attention and this powder room is a perfect illustration of a small space with a big personality. Just because a space is utilitarian doesn't mean it can't be interesting!

WHAT MAKES THIS SPACE FAMILY FRIENDLY?

The most unique feature of this space is the exact thing that makes it perfect for a family. The floor—created with actual nickels—is both different and practical all at the same time.

WHAT FEARS NEED TO BE OVERCOME?

Thinking outside of the box can cause trepidation. Using actual nickels to create a floor might seem crazy to some, but that doesn't mean it really is.

WHAT COMPROMISE IS REQUIRED?

Sealed like tile, the nickels provide a cost-effective (only about ninety dollars!) and sturdy flooring that gives a creative flavor to the space. From a distance, they look like normal "penny" tiles. It's not until they are studied that their uniqueness is revealed. So rather than asking "why" . . . the real question should be "why not?"

BORROW *This* IDEA

USE UNEXPECTED MATERIALS TO give your space personal flair. You don't have to use coins to create flooring. Try using a tree branch as a curtain rod or a colander as a light fixture. Everyday objects given new life can add whimsical flavor to your home.

A COLOR PALETTE LIMITED PRIMARILY TO BLACK
AND WHITE MAKES THIS HOUSE CLEAN, CRISP, AND
UNIFIED. PRETTY DETAILS LIKE PLANK PANELING
AND SUBWAY TILE LEND DEPTH AND INTEREST.
THE HOMEOWNER GREW UP IN THIS HOUSE BUT
HAS GIVEN IT A FRESH FACE-LIFT THAT MAKES IT
PERFECT FOR ANOTHER GENERATION.

CLEAN & CONTEMPORARY

GREAT
ROOM

WHAT DOES THIS SPACE SAY?

We're a family that loves spending time together. And this wide open space makes togetherness easy!

WHAT MAKES THIS SPACE FAMILY FRIENDLY?

Comfortable seating, a plush ottoman-turned-coffee-table, and an oversize kitchen island combine to make a functional great room perfect for living life with a boisterous family of boys. Clever touches like a barn-door pantry and industrial lighting make the space feel current but timeless all at once.

WHAT FEARS NEED TO BE OVERCOME?

Restricting a home's color palette can feel limiting, but it actually provides a great deal of decorating freedom.

WHAT COMPROMISE IS REQUIRED?

By choosing a color palette with a lot of contrast, such as black and white, this homeowner has opened up her options in a unique way. A variety of bold patterns can easily be incorporated into the space as long as they are consistent in color. A black wall creates a dramatic focal point for displaying family photos that likely would not have the same impact in any other color. When other colors are added in small pops, they have a greater effect than they might otherwise have, giving the homeowner the ability to more vividly change the feeling of the space with less investment.

BORROW *This* IDEA

CONSIDER A BARN DOOR. In spaces where a traditional door might be awkward, adding a barn door can be just the ticket to increasing the usability of a room. The only limiting factor is whether or not there is enough wall space to install the hardware. Make sure that the space next to the doorway in question is at least as wide as the door itself. If the room is sufficient, then adding a barn door can be a perfect—and stylish—solution for a tight space.

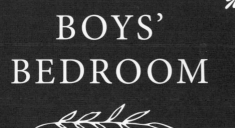

BOYS'
BEDROOM

WHAT DOES THIS SPACE SAY?

We love imaginative adventures and cozy hiding places. This bedroom offers both!

WHAT MAKES THIS SPACE FAMILY FRIENDLY?

Built-in bunk beds are a perfect solution for smaller bedrooms. The addition of book niches and light sconces for each bed, as well as privacy curtains, gives each boy the chance to have a space all his own. A nautical theme is incorporated with the choice of fabrics, finishes, and accessories, giving the room a feeling of discovery. And during daylight hours, the beds make perfect forts for hours of pretend play!

WHAT FEARS NEED TO BE OVERCOME?

Giving a theme to a room can be nerve-wracking, but it can also pay off in a big way.

WHAT COMPROMISE IS REQUIRED?

Themed rooms can be great—especially when decorating for children. But going over the top with a theme simply creates more work in the end as children tend to move rapidly from interest to interest, which causes the space to become dated quickly. Take a cue from this room and incorporate themes with subtlety. A bit of fabric, a pillow, and an accessory might be all it takes to give flavor to a space without all-out commitment.

BORROW *This* IDEA

VINTAGE CLASSROOM MAPS MAKE great art. Search online for vintage charts and maps and you're sure to find a deal. You don't have to limit such items to children's rooms, however. Botanical, entomological, and other scientific charts make interesting art pieces in about any room of the house.

FAMILY ROOM

WHAT DOES THIS SPACE SAY?

A rough-and-tumble space with durable finishes is a great place for our family to play games and watch the latest movies!

WHAT MAKES THIS SPACE FAMILY FRIENDLY?

Faux wood tile makes perfect flooring for this basement family room. Area rugs warm up and soften the space for little knees that gather around the coffee table. Comfortable throws on the white slipcover sofas protect areas that tend to collect dirt the fastest and remain close at hand for snuggling up to watch a movie.

WHAT FEARS NEED TO BE OVERCOME?

Creating a living space in a basement brings its own set of challenges. Lack of light and fear of water infiltration can be daunting obstacles.

WHAT COMPROMISE IS REQUIRED?

In this basement, the homeowners opted for a tile floor that looks like wood rather than using actual wood flooring or carpet. If there should be any basement flooding, the tile floor is much less likely to be damaged.

To combat a lack of light, bright white walls and pale colored furnishings work to make the space feel bright despite its subterranean location.

BORROW *This* IDEA

CREATE A MULTIFUNCTIONAL SPACE with built-in shelves. Adding floating shelves to the awkward spaces on either side of this fireplace gave the homeowners extra storage and display space along with desk space for homework or writing a note.

FURNITURE
LAYOUT TOOLS

USE THE FURNITURE TEMPLATES AND GRAPH
PAPER ON THE FOLLOWING PAGES TO HELP
WORK OUT SPACE PLANNING DETAILS.

FURNITURE TEMPLATES

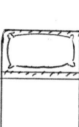

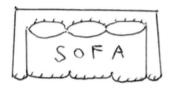

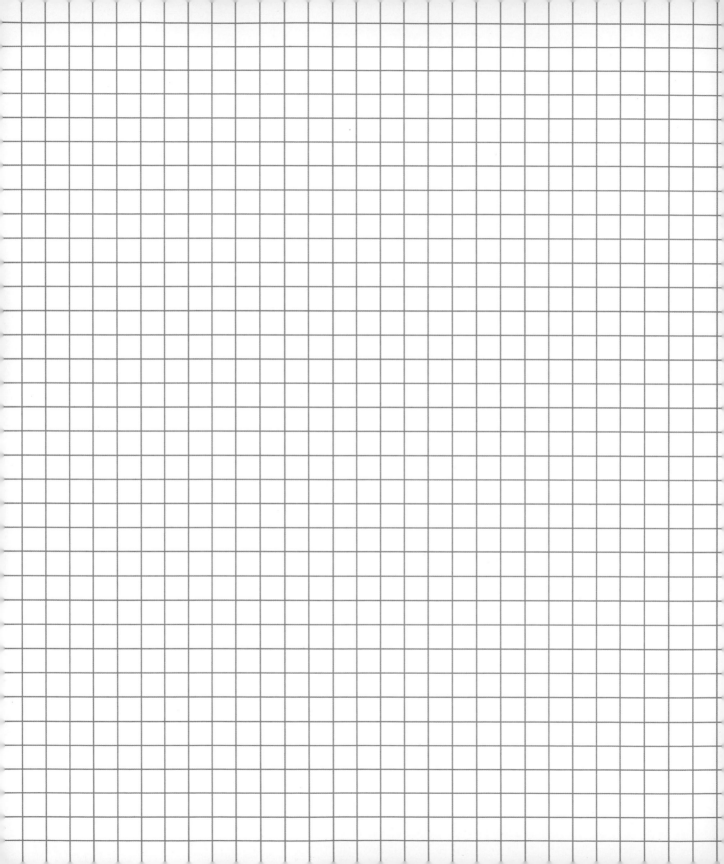

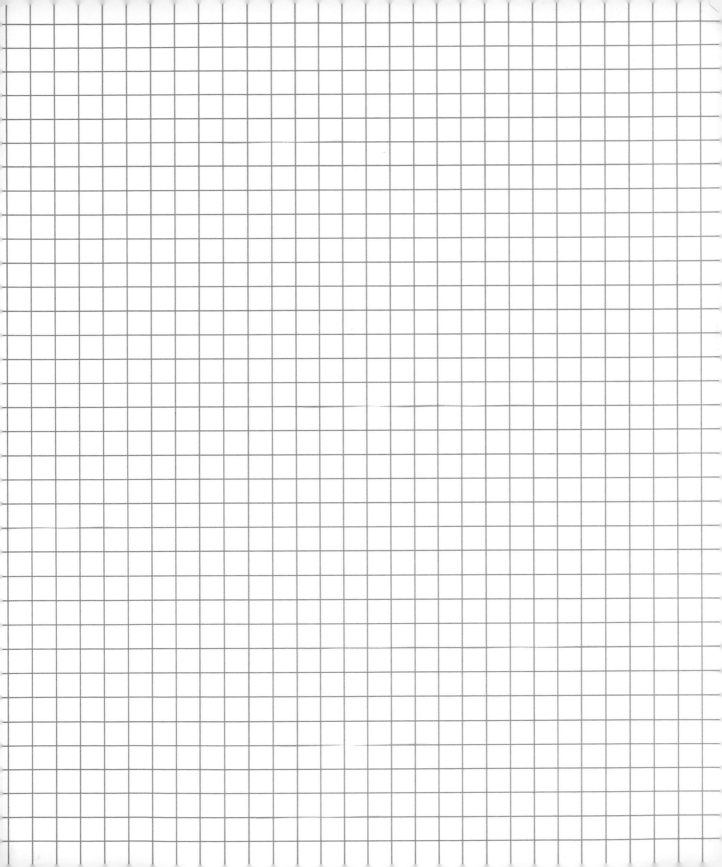

RESOURCES & INSPIRATION

CONTRIBUTORS BLOGS & WEBSITES

Aly Brooks
Entirely Eventful, **entirelyeventfulday.com**

Anne-Marie Barton
annemariebarton.com

Autumn Clemons
Design Dump, **mydesigndump.blogspot.com**

Jennifer Hadfield
Tatertots & Jello, **tatertotsandjello.com**

Megan Hobson
Megan Hobson Photography, **meganhobsonphoto.com**

Michelle Hinckley
4 Men 1 Lady, **4men1lady.com**

Paige Knudsen
Paige Knudsen Photography, **paigeknudsen.com**

Shelley Smith
The House of Smiths, **thehouseofsmiths.com**

Wendy Hyde
The Shabby Nest, **shabbynest.blogspot.com**

OTHER HELPFUL & INSPIRATIONAL SITES

Waterlogue App
Used to create the beautiful watercolors featured in this book. **waterlogueapp.com**

Roomstyler
A free online furniture arranging tool. **austin.roomstyler.com/rooms/austin**

Houzz
An online resource for creating your own inspiration files. **houzz.com**

PHOTOGRAPHERS

MEGAN HOBSON

ALL PHOTOGRAPHY BY MEGAN HOBSON
UNLESS OTHERWISE NOTED

MEGAN HOBSON is a fine art photographer based out of Utah. Growing up around art and design, she was raised with an appreciation for the beauty and simplicity of aesthetics in the world. She graduated with her Bachelors of Fine Art in photography from Brigham Young University–Idaho after discovering her passion for photography. Her work has been shown in the BYU–Idaho Spori Art Gallery, the Springville Museum of Art, and the Alpine Art Gallery.

meganhobsonphoto.com

PAIGE KNUDSEN

PHOTOGRAPHY OF SIMPLE AND SERENE, PAGES 131–43

PAIGE KNUDSEN is a former pediatric nurse turned lifestyle blogger, self-taught photographer, and ambassador for Noonday Collection. Born and raised in the South, she's currently raising four daughters with her husband along with an old-soul golden retriever outside of Atlanta, Georgia.

paigeknudsen.com

ACKNOWLEDGMENTS

WRITING A BOOK has been number one on my bucket list since I was a little girl. Having the opportunity to write a book about my passion is literally a dream come true. I have loved interior design since I was young and I need to start by thanking my parents for giving me free reign to decorate my bedroom in any way I saw fit. Thank you for letting me paint my walls purple. Thank you for building furniture for me. Thank for you loving me and believing in me and helping me believe in myself. Mom, you always told me I could do anything I put my mind to. Dad, I always knew I could count on you to create the visions in my head with wood. I couldn't have asked for better parents. I love you.

To my beautiful children, a sincere thank you for putting up with me while I was writing this book. Thank you for letting me work on the book when it would have been more fun to go to the movies. Thank you for giving me hugs, telling me you love me, and lending me your exuberance. You are my angels and my greatest achievements. I love you all to the moon and back!

To my sisters, Holly and Kelly, you are my biggest cheerleaders and I love you more than words can express. Thank you for our long talks and for not thinking I'm crazy even when I might be. You are my best friends. And to my brother Warren, I miss you every day. You have a beautiful spirit and I am grateful for the years we had together.

To the DIY Divas, I simply can't thank you enough for all of your support and expertise. Thank you for teaching me so much, for challenging me, and for making me dare to try new things! I will forever be grateful to the world of blogging for bringing us together. You are amazing and beautiful ladies and I love each and every one of you.

To all the incredible homeowners that shared their beautiful spaces in this book, I am in awe of each of you and your talent and general awesomeness. Megan, Kara, Aly, Shelley, Jen, Michelle, Anne-Marie, Autumn, Paige, and Rowena—I couldn't have done this without you!

To Megan, thank you for lending me your amazing talent. You have a true gift, and I am so blessed to know you and to have had the opportunity to work with you on this project. We make a good creative team!

To Kara, thank you for asking me to decorate your home even though the install lasted until four a.m. Thank you for being hilarious, going on diet coke runs with me, making cheesecake for my birthday and *thank you* especially for talking me into red hair.

ACKNOWLEDGMENTS

To Aly, my supermodel blogging bestie. Thank you for letting me toss around book titles with you. Thank you for painting oversize canvases for me. And thank you for dancing like we were teenagers with me in Atlanta. It was a blast!

To Shelley, thank you for your infectious laugh and your joyous spirit.

To Jen, thank you for your gentleness and willingness to share your adorable cottage.

To Michelle, thank you for trying valiantly to find me a cell-phone charging cord and for talking blogging shop with me.

To Anne-Marie, thank you for sharing your story with me and your beautiful home with my readers.

To Autumn, thank you for wandering into the showroom one day and for being willing to tell me about your "strange" e-design job. We are kindred spirits, you and I.

To Paige, your blog was one of the first I ever read. Thank you for inspiring me with your beautiful photography and your love for your family. I loved chatting with you over a real Southern breakfast!

To Rowena, thank you for your enthusiasm and your amazing eye. I am so grateful our paths crossed in Massachusetts. You are an amazing woman!

Thank you to Stephanie for my lovely blog design and branding.

And thank you to the wonderful team at Cedar Fort Publishing for giving me the amazing opportunity to write this book. You have all been a pleasure to work with!

INDEX

ABOUT THE AUTHOR

WENDY HYDE is passionate about interior design and equally passionate about sharing design inspiration with those around her. In 2008, she started writing her blog, *The Shabby Nest*, in an effort to connect with like-minded design lovers. In 2011, *The Shabby Nest* was chosen as the best decorating blog of the year by *Country Living Magazine*. Since then, Wendy has appeared as a speaker at home and garden shows, on both local and national television shows, in local newspapers, and in national magazines sharing her design ideas and DIY know-how with the public.

Having studied both fashion and interior design, Wendy brings a unique perspective to her work. One of her readers once told Wendy that she had "an eye for pretty." That phrase resonated with her and has become a guiding principle both on her blog and in her daily design work. In addition to writing her blog, Wendy works as an interior designer for Utah home builder, Ivory Homes. She loves helping her clients create beautiful spaces that they will be happy to call home.

Wendy and her four children live in a cozy home in Utah where they enjoy creative pursuits, laughing with one another, and redecorating . . . a lot.

PHOTOGRAPHY BY JOHN HYDE